In Pursuit of Success and Happiness:
A Practical Guide

By

Dr. Darryl Cross

By the same Author:

You're a New Leader: So Now What?

Listen up Now: How to Increase Growth and Profit by Really Listening to Your Customers and Clients

Stopping Your Self-Sabotage: Steps to Increase Self-Confidence

The Dark Clouds at Work: How to Manage Depressed Staff in the Workplace Whilst Increasing Morale and Productivity

Growing up Children: How To Get 5-12 Year Olds To Behave & Do As They're Told

Teenager Trouble-shooting: How to Stop Your Adolescent Driving You Crazy

**Available as an audio-book on
<u>www.SuccessPursuit.com</u> or <u>www.DrDarryl.com</u> :**

Cover design by Nu-Image Design

Published by Crossways Publishing

ISBN:
0-9806101-2-5

ISBN-13:
978-0-9806101-2-3

Disclaimer

This publication is designed to provide accurate and authoritative information with regard to the subject matter covered. It is sold with the understanding that the author is not engaged in rendering legal, accounting or financial advice of any kind. If legal advice, advice relating to mental health issues or any other professional assistance is required, the services of a competent professional in the appropriate area should be sought.

The author denies any liability for incidental or consequential damages resulting from the use of the information in this book. This book is designed to assist with generating and exploring various options for increasing happiness and fulfilment in life. It does not make decisions for the individual, but provides a range of options to be considered. No responsibility is accepted for any liabilities resulting from the actions of any parties involved.

Acknowledgements

I am indebted to Rev Craig Broman who initially asked me to present to a group of people from his City Workers' Ministry on the general topic of happiness. That began a journey not only in researching this field, but in compiling what anecdotally I had been sharing and learning with my clients over more than three decades. This book is the outcome of that journey.

My thanks to all those clients who I have had the privilege of meeting professionally who have taught me so much about life and the pursuit of success and happiness. We all have so much to learn.

I am grateful for the assistance afforded by both Richard Banham and Viano Jaksa in their ability to use software and particularly in relation to formatting issues which can be the bane of almost everyone's life at times. I am thankful too that both are Apple fans. Thanks to Gwen Hoffnagle for all her diligent work in proof-reading and editing. Her continued attention to detail and her efficiency in meeting deadlines was refreshing as was her pleasant and cooperative manner.

I am indebted too to my wife Billie who continues to encourage and support and who understands that there are times when I am laptop bound.

Darryl

Contents

CHAPTER 1

Introduction

Ask anyone what they'd like in life and generally it's to be happy. Of course some say that they'd like things like their health or to win the lottery, but almost without exception they're expressing the desire to be happy.

This pursuit of happiness has long been at the centre of theories about human behaviour and experience, but in today's time-poor, cash-rich, material wealth society, it's almost become an obsession. Certainly, we've seen many gurus, experts, coaches and psychologists emerge, each with their own particular brand of how to increase our happiness.

However, a tipping point came in 1998 with Professor Martin Seligman who as incoming President of the American Psychological Association rallied the profession to concentrate on "positive psychology". It was indeed a turning point for the way that psychologists approached their work. Instead of focusing on mental illness and the down side of life, Seligman challenged psychologists to study ways to make healthy people even better.

The whole notion caught on – and why wouldn't it? As New York journalist Barbara Ehrenreich says in her book *"Smile or Die,"* "They started thinking, well, what about those people who aren't sick or neurotic right now but who are just going about their lives?"

Happiness is a bit like money, beauty or success – even those who have an abundance usually want more. Not surprisingly, positive psychology became a dominant force and the staple of such TV talk shows like *Oprah* and *Dr Phil*.

Interestingly, not only was it psychologists that turned their attention to positive psychology and happiness, but so did governments. Various governing bodies around the world have started to look at ways to increase the happiness and well-being of their populations.

As Professor Felicia Huppert from the University of Cambridge reported at the Second Australian Positive Psychology Conference in Melbourne in February 2010, during December 2009, policy makers and researchers from more than 100 countries met at Iguazu Falls in Brazil for the Fifth International Gross National Happiness Conference. This notion came from the tiny kingdom of Bhutan in the Himalayas which has legislated that happiness be a consideration in all policy making. Bhutan's monarch has been reported as stating that, "Gross National Happiness is more important than Gross National Product." Talk about setting the trend for the rest of us!

Having said that, we do need to understand though that there is no linear relationship between happiness and GDP. In Britain, people are now three times wealthier than in the 1950s, but the proportion of people who say that they are "very happy" has fallen from 52% to 36%. In China, between 1999-2000, there was a strong push to pull people out of poverty and while the Gross Domestic Product increased 400%, happiness actually decreased.

In the 2019 World Happiness Report, a survey of 156 countries by the United Nations, Australia's happiness ranking dropped from 10th to 11th place. Finland is the happiest country in the world, followed by Denmark, Norway and Iceland. The United Kingdom rated 15th and the USA was 19th.

Regardless, happiness is a universal need, irrespective of culture or creed. It just seems that everyone wants to be happy. So what is this happiness thing and how do you get it?

What is Happiness?

For most of us happiness means something like a lack of stress, a lack of feeling stretched, or even a lack of distress. Maybe it means being wealthy or out of debt. It might mean having freedom and independence.

Actually, there are five major emotions that deprive us of our happiness. In other words, if we're not happy, then there is a very high probability that we'll be feeling one (or more) of these five major emotions. What do you think those five major negative emotions might be?

- Anxiety (we use words like "stressed", "up-tight", "tense", "scared" etc.)
- Depression (we use words like, "feeling down", "feeling blue", "feeling flat" etc.)
- Anger (we use words like, "annoyed", "ticked off", "irritated" etc.)
- Guilt (we use words like, "guilty", "ashamed", "embarrassed" etc.)
- Resentment (we use words like "resentful", "bitter" etc.)

The top three are the big three. Drug companies make their money from the top two – anxiety and depression. Anger, of course, is widespread in our community, and we see it played out each day in the media in the form of violence, assault and aggression. We now have road rage, supermarket queue rage, and even desk rage. (Yes, those computers can really get us steaming!) In relation to guilt, though, it needs to be said that some guilt is worthwhile and important. If you are stealing the firm's stationery, for instance, you ought to feel guilty and change your behaviour. However, many of us feel guilty needlessly, such as when we are unable to attend a friend's party because we already had a trip planned, or when we cancel coffee with a friend because we have other deadlines to meet.

By the way, of these five emotions, which one would you say is the most powerful? In other words, which one is the most destructive? Resentment. In my opinion, resentment is the big one, because resentment will ultimately kill you. It's a destructive emotion that stays with an individual for a long time, and over that time period it becomes like an emotional cancer. It's the emotion that is at the core of family members not talking to each other, sometimes for decades. It's the emotion behind feuds, behind wars. If you have resentment in your life, get rid of it. You will do yourself a big favour. (The next chapter covers how to do this is more detail.) Resentment certainly destroys happiness. Big time.

Happiness though, is not the brief burst of pleasure afforded by chocolate, alcohol, sex, or buying that fabulous wide-screen television. It's more than that. It's a deep and ongoing mood state, a lasting sense of well-being. This doesn't mean though that people don't experience bad days, it just means that such are not the norm.

Happiness is about feeling a sense of satisfaction, a sense of joy, and a sense of peace. **Happiness is defined as a state of mind or feeling such as contentment, satisfaction, or joy.** The ABC's national medical reporter, Sophie Scott has said in her book, *"Roadtesting Happiness"* that it's more akin to "something where you have the ability to feel fulfilled and able to cope with the challenges of life. It's not just pleasurable experiences like a nice dinner, but something that adds an extra dimension and meaning".

"You're addicted to thrills?
What an empty life!
The pursuit of pleasure is never satisfied."

Proverbs 21:17

A variety of philosophical, religious, psychological and biological approaches have been taken to defining happiness and identifying its sources.

Philosophers and religious thinkers have often defined happiness in terms of living a good life, or flourishing, rather than simply as an emotion. *Happiness,* in this older sense, reflects the meaning of the Greek word, eudaimonia, and is still used in virtue ethics. Eudaimonia combines the Greek words for "well-being" and "spirit" or "minor deity" to mean good fortune.

In everyday speech today, however, terms such as **well-being** and **quality of life** are usually used to signify the classical meaning.

The Genes Have It In Part

What you need to know too is that your genes have a good deal to play in your happiness. Yes, you can blame mother and father for some things in life!

One of the findings that researchers have been telling us for decades is that with IQ for example, it's largely determined by our parents. Around 60-70% of your intelligence comes from your genes and then peaks around your mid-twenties and it's largely downhill from there. (That's not quite true however, when we see more recent research and reviews from people like psychiatrist Dr Norman Doidge who says quite clearly in his book *"The Brain that Changes Itself"* that the brain is very plastic (called neuro-plasticity) where we can, in fact, alter and improve our IQ.)

Nevertheless, when it comes to happiness, University of Minnesota Professor Emeritus of Psychology and Psychiatry David Lykken concluded in 1996 that about 50% of one's satisfaction with life comes from genetic programming. In other words, **half of our happiness apparently comes from our genes**. Lykken, who died in 2006, was famous for gathering data on 4,000 sets of twins born in Minnesota from 1936 through to 1955. After comparing happiness data on identical versus fraternal twins, he came to the conclusion that our genes influence such traits as having a sunny, easy-going personality; dealing well with stress; and feeling low levels of anxiety and depression. Lykken found that circumstantial factors like income, marital status, religion and education contribute only about 8% to our overall well-being.

Hence, because of the relatively large influence of our genes, Lykken proposed the idea that our mood is regulated around an optimal level called a **"set point"**. An easy way to understand this is to compare it to another bodily function that works in largely the say way, our body temperature. Having a high or low body temperature will put stress on out body over time, so it's preferable to have an optimal set-point temperature of 37 degree Celsius. It actually takes effort and energy to maintain a higher or lower level of happiness, so our body works hard to bring us back to our optimal level. No matter what happens in our life – good, bad, spectacular, tragic – we tend to return in short order to our set range a bit like the automatic pilot returns a plane to its original set path.

However, this is not to be taken as bad news. The flip side is that even if around 50% of our happiness is attributable to our heredity, and around 8% is due to external factors like income and so on, *that still leaves about 42% that is up for grabs!*

As Dr Sonja Lyubomirsky from the University of California reported at the Happiness and Its Causes

Conference in Sydney, her research shows that it was possible to increase a person's level of happiness over their natural set point. "If people desire greater happiness, they need to invest as much time and effort in their emotional life as they do in their bodies." Wise words, and common sense really.

It's a Process not an Outcome

Happiness and success are ongoing endeavours, and you never really arrive. I wish I could tell you that there is an end point, a spot that you could aim for, and that you will some day get there and say, "I've made it", but it "ain't necessarily so". **It's a journey; it's a process.** Having said that, there are certainly things that you can do to promote more happiness and fulfilment in your life. No doubt about it.

What we're looking for as a society today are tips about that journey, tips about how we can be more happy than not, more successful than not. Human kind has always been on the search for a happier lifestyle, however, the search in more recent times seems to have intensified. The search for the easier lifestyle, the retired life, the relaxed holiday adventures all abound. Why so? We can only speculate, but what is clear is that stress levels in the community have significantly increased over the last few decades. Some researchers such as Dr. Craig Hassed from the Department of General Practice at Monash University in Victoria, Australia have suggested that stress levels have gone up by 45% since the mid-1970s.

One certain area of stress for many is the daily commute to work. Repeated studies have examined the link between commute time and a poor quality of life. One in particular found that people who commute for longer than 40 minutes each day are unhappier, more stressed and generally experience more worry than those who have only a 10-minute commute. In fact, the HILDA (Household, Income and Labour Dynamics in Australia) Survey in 2019 showed that commute times have blown out by 23 percent over the last 15 years and have big influence on job satisfaction. Not surprisingly too, the long daily commute is also placing strain on work-family balance which is another prime factor in the happiness equation. HILDA data showed that in 68% of couples with children under 18, and where both partners work, work-family balance was a key. Those working 55 or more hours a week recognised they were missing out on family activities as well as having too little time or energy for parenting. Among couples where both report high work-family conflict, 2.5% separate within the next year compared to 1.6% where both partners have low work-family conflict.

Someone once wrote, "Most people live in survival, not in fulfilment". Let me say it again for those who may have missed it! Most people live in survival, not in fulfilment. The challenge today is how to actually move towards fulfilment; how do we get that? How do we strive for that? What does it mean?

It was the writer and philosopher Henry David Thoreau who said that, "Most men lead lives of quiet desperation and go to the grave with the song still in them". How do we break out of our desperation and how do we learn to sing? Really sing.

Life is full of paradoxes. The Bible, for example, highlights a number of these paradoxes. When someone says that you need to lose your life in order to find it, most people say, "What? Run that past me again." Here's another: If you want to get, you've got to give. For example, if you want to receive love, then give it. There are lots of back-to-front rules, and those are a couple of them. Here's another rule: Good things take time. There's no way around that. There are no quick fixes and the road to happiness does take time as we learn the lessons of life.

I'm reminded of a cartoon that I saw once with the character Hagar, the Viking. The scene shows Hagar climbing up the mountain to consult the wise monk at the top and he asks the question, "What is the key to happiness?" The wise monk dressed in dark flowing robes and attire, looks solemnly down at Hagar and replies, "Abstinence, poverty, fasting and celibacy." Hagar ponders a moment and then asks, "Is there someone else up there I could talk to?"

Not always is the news that we receive, the news we want to hear. Sometimes too, we need to un-learn that which we already "know". Perhaps we need to take a fresh look at things.

"For things to change,
I first must change."

Tony Robbins

A Quick Overview

So what are the strategies for increasing our sense of pleasure and our sense of fulfilment? **What has science learned about what makes the human heart sing?** More than one might imagine, along with some surprising things about **what doesn't ring our inner chimes.**

For example, what **doesn't do** it for us is:

• **Wealth**, and all the delightful things that money can buy; a study of lottery winners done in 1978 found, for instance, that they did not wind up significantly happier than a control group.

Research by University of Illinois psychologist Edward Diener (a.k.a. Dr. Happiness) has shown that once your basic needs are met, additional income does little to raise your sense of satisfaction with life. In the UK, University of Cambridge Professor Felicia Huppert reports that satisfaction in life increases up to £45,000 and then there is a slackening off. In Australia, Dr Michael Mosley told the 2019 "Happiness and Its Causes Conference" that in Australia, the minimum wage to be relatively happy is about $50,000 and the maximum point at which you get satiated where actually having more money won't make you happier is $90,000.

However, there is apparently another level of happiness when you feel that you've "made it" and that turns out to be about $140,000. This is consistent with Professor Bob Cummins from Deakin University who states that the threshold is about $125,000 to $150,000 because once you get there, you have essentially bought your way out of all the things that you can buy your way out of. In other words, once you've bought yourself out of trouble, extra money does not contribute to increased happiness.

- **A good education**; sorry, Mum and Dad, neither education nor, for that matter, a high IQ paves the road to happiness. It's not so much what's above the neck-line that counts nor the piece of paper or qualification, it's more about what's below the neck-line with your character and personality.

- **Youth**; no, again. In fact, older people are more consistently satisfied with their lives than the young. And they're less prone to dark moods. A recent survey by the Center for Disease Control and Prevention found that people aged 20 to 24 are sad for an average of 3.4

days a month, as opposed to just 2.3 days for people aged 65 to 74. Similarly, Dr Maria Hennessy, a senior lecturer in psychology at James Cook University in Queensland states that her research shows that the older you grow, the happier you become.

Once people reach 40, their sense of happiness begins to recover. She suggests that people in their 50s however, could be undergoing a change in life perspective where they are leaving behind all the angst from their 20s with the rush of marriage, careers and children and are able to sit down and get more comfortable with their lives and where they want to go. A report in *The Economist* indicates that by the time people reach 70, they feel just as happy as they did as a young person.

- **Marriage**; a complicated picture – married people are generally happier than singles, but that may be because they were happier to begin with.

- **The Weather and Sunny days**; nope, although a 1998 study showed that Midwesterners in the USA think folks living in balmy California are happier and that Californians incorrectly believe this about themselves, too.

Although we will discuss this in more detail later, here are just **three positive things that do** make our hearts sing:

- **Religious faith** seems to genuinely lift the spirit. It's not certain though whether it's the faith in God part or the supportive community aspect that does the heavy lifting, or perhaps both.

- **Friends and relationships**; a giant yes. A 2002 study conducted at the University of Illinois by Diener and Seligman found that the most salient characteristics shared by the 10% of students with the highest levels of happiness and the fewest signs of depression were their strong ties to friends and family and their commitment to spending time with them. Similarly, the World Happiness Report in 2019 found that the greatest single predictor of whether someone is happy or not is whether they had relatives or fiends that could help them in times of trouble or need. In other words, it is important to work on social skills, close interpersonal ties and social support in order to be happy.

- **Health**; there's a developing literature which reveals that people who are thriving in life experience better physical health. They take less sick days, see the doctor less, and need less time off than people who are languishing physically. Activity and staying in a healthy weight range contribute to positive mental health.

So let's explore in more detail what the research and clinical findings suggest really makes us happy and leads us towards a life of success.

Chapter 1 Summary

The desire for happiness is universal. While we strive in all sorts of ways to be happy, research shows that around 50% of our happiness is pre-determined via our genes. A further 8% of happiness is related to our income, marital status, religion and education. However, that still leaves around 42% up for grabs!

But happiness is a process rather than a destination, and it's illusive to many. Sadly, most people though live in survival mode instead of in fulfilment.

Anxiety, depression, anger, guilt and resentment are the major roadblocks to happiness, which instead, can be likened to a sense of satisfaction, joy, peace, and contentment; the ability to feel fulfilled and able to cope with the challenges of life.

In short, religious faith, connection with others and good physical health have all been shown to contribute the most to happiness.

"Life will bring you pain all by itself.
Your responsibility is to create joy."

Author unknown

CHAPTER 2

Deal with the Past

It's difficult to be happy or to seek to be happy if you're carrying baggage from the past. It's like going on a journey with a very heavy back-pack. Sure, you may be fine initially, but you'll tire fast, become fatigued, and find the going very tough. If you're travelling along with others, you'll find that they will overtake you, and you'll fall behind. You'll become despondent and lose energy.

It's just like that with emotional baggage. There are two big emotional loads that you don't want to have to carry into your present and your future, and they both start with "R" – Regret and Resentment. There is absolutely no doubt that these two are guaranteed to rob you of your happiness and your success in life. You need to dump your "stuff".

1. Regret – What is Over is Over

You can't change what is over. It's spilled milk. The difficulty for many of us, though, is that we keep beating up on ourselves about our spilled milk. We deny our happiness because we say things like, "If only..." and we lament what we said or did or didn't say or do. There's no point berating yourself. However, the loudest voice you'll ever hear is certainly your own. I always thought the loudest voices when I was young were Mom and Dad when they were stark raving mad at me, but not true. The loudest voice I ever hear is really my own. I beat up on myself much more than anyone else can beat up on me. Is that how it is for you? But what's over is over. There's no point berating yourself. Be kind to yourself. Don't live a life of regret.

"The biggest myth in education and life is that we're not allowed to make mistakes – yet making mistakes is the basis of learning."

Darryl Cross

The real issue though, once it's all over, is to ask ourselves what we learned, because life is about making mistakes and learning from them. Every mistake is an opportunity to learn.

*"Only those who dare to fail greatly, can
ever achieve greatly."*

Robert F. Kennedy

Anyone I've ever met on the planet – and I've met a lot of people whose lives I've been privileged to share, both as a coach and as a psychologist – has made mistakes. No one has had a dream run. Those who are successful have made the most mistakes, but they usually don't make the same mistake twice. They don't make the same mistakes over and over. What is over is over. Move on and don't be tied to the past.

*"We learn wisdom from failure much more
than from success."*

Author unknown

2. Resentment – Forgiveness is the Fragrance

Mark Twain once wrote, *"Forgiveness is the fragrance that the violet sheds on the heel that has crushed it."*

From the psychologist's point of view, it is probably true to say that forgiving is often the most important thing that clients need to do. Forgive. Forgive a friend who wronged you, forgive a boss who bullied you, forgive a parent who abused you, forgive a partner who betrayed you, forgive a neighbour who cheated you, forgive a teacher who put you down, forgive a sibling who upset you.

Why bother with forgiveness? Isn't it just a bit "old hat", or maybe just a bit too religious?

I once heard a story about a large, somewhat obvious sign which hung behind the desk of a typically tough U.S. Marine major. The sign read, "To err is human; to forgive is divine – and our policy is to do neither!" Interesting comment indeed. But what's our own "policy" when it comes to forgiveness? We certainly know what it is to err, to do something that we're not proud of, to overstep the line. But what about forgiving? What does forgiveness really imply, and should we be interested in promoting this virtue for others around us and for ourselves?

"Forgiveness does not change the past,
but it does enlarge the future."

Paul Boese

Consider how a snake bite kills. In the same way, refusing to forgive others is like venom in your thoughts which you carry with you and which ultimately destroys you.

We make up rules inside our heads about how people **should** react and behave towards us and others. When they "break" those rules, we get upset (or annoyed, resentful, frustrated, angry, etc.). Perhaps we often play it cool and are aloof; we sulk, we withdraw and we give the other person(s) a hard time.

But really, in a nutshell, feeling resentful towards others for breaking our rules is ridiculous. Somehow or other, we believe that we can punish others by refusing to forgive them. "If I don't forgive you, you suffer."

Know what? Actually, **it's us who suffer.** We're the ones who feel tense. It's our stomachs that churn. We're the ones who lose sleep. We're the ones who feel fatigued. We're the ones who get headaches. We're the ones who feel miserable.

So, what's the answer? This is not a cop-out, but the answer is within you. Don't punish yourself by trying to punish someone else. It's futile. It's senseless. Give up trying to make others feel badly. Take charge of yourself. Let it all go. Silently forgive. Carry a clean plate. Where do you need to offer yourself a clean plate? To whom do you need to offer a clean plate?

What is Forgiveness?

Forgiveness entails a series of changes that occur within an individual who has been offended or hurt in some way by another person. In other words, **you**

choose to forgive. You make a decision. You make a choice. Forgiveness cannot be coerced, but must be freely chosen by the one who was wronged.

When individuals forgive, their thoughts and actions toward the transgressor become more positive (e.g., more peaceful and more compassionate) and less negative (e.g., less wrathful and less avoiding).

How Do You Learn to Forgive?

Remember I said earlier that you need to forget about the past. Let go of it. Let go of anger and resentment, perhaps by writing a letter, or sincerely apologising to someone who has hurt you or who has wronged you. Hanging on to it actually causes you to suffer. I know that that's painful to hear, and it's painful to feel too, but it's you who suffers when you hang on to resentment and to anger. It only hurts you.

Developmental psychologist Robert Enright provided a process model of forgiveness in the *Chronicle of Higher Education,* in 1998, in which he outlined the following **nine steps** towards forgiveness:

1. **Acknowledge your emotions.** Whether you are angry, hurt, ashamed or embarrassed (or some combination of the above), acknowledge your emotional reaction to the wrongdoing. Name the feeling.

2. Go beyond identifying the person who hurt you, and instead **articulate or identify the specific behaviours that upset or hurt you**.

3. **Make the choice to forgive**. Remember, forgiveness is a choice, a decision. You don't have to *feel* like it, you just have to do it.

4. **Explain to yourself why you made the decision to forgive**. Your reasons can be as practical as wanting to be free of the anger so that you can concentrate on more important things. Maybe it will be like getting a monkey off your back, and being able to breathe again.

5. **Attempt to "walk in the shoes" of the other person**. Consider that person's vulnerabilities. What's their situation? What might have prompted them to act in the way that they did? This is not to excuse their behaviour, but to understand it better.

6. **Make a commitment to not pass along the pain you have endured** – even to the person who hurt you in the first place and certainly not to others. Why should others wear your resentment, annoyance or grumpiness?

7. **Decide instead to offer the world mercy and good will**. In other words, at this stage, you may wish to reconcile with the other person, but that's

not necessary. You may, instead, write out a note of forgiveness – expressing how you feel and then expressing forgiveness to the other person – then burn the note. I've even had clients bury the note, but burning it seems to be more of a final act. But it's important to do something.

8. **Reflect on how it feels to let go of a grudge**. Find meaning in the suffering you experienced and overcame. Feel the strength that comes from forgiving and letting go.

9. **Discover the paradox of forgiveness**. As you give the gift of forgiveness to someone, you receive the gift of peace. It's a back to front rule, but life is full of such rules as we've said earlier.

Forgiving Ourselves

Forgiving yourself is critical too. Philosopher André Comte-Sponville once said the following:

"Can one forgive oneself? Of course, since one can hate oneself and overcome self-hatred. What hope would there be for wisdom otherwise? Or for happiness? Or for peace? We must forgive ourselves for being merely what we are. And also forgive ourselves – when we can do so without injustice – for feeling hatred or pain or anger so strong that we cannot forgive. Fortunate are the merciful, who fight without hatred or hate without remorse!"

Living without forgiving yourself would be like living with an inner torment, an inner torture. Why would you do that? Do you think that you are so bad that you can't be forgiven, or that what you've done can't be forgiven?

In the Christian tradition, forgiving yourself frequently means "repenting". Repentance has three components. A failure to make genuine change and transformation results when we have failed at one of the 3Rs of repentance:

Recognise: Identify that you are doing something you don't want to do. Without awareness, we will never recognise our need to change. Self-awareness is the cornerstone of change.

Regret: Be conscious of the cost of your actions to others and to yourself. If we don't truly regret our actions, we will not change.

Reorient: Turn from what you don't want, to what you do want. If we continue to focus our attention on what we don't want, we will persist in that behaviour.

Interestingly, the failure to reorient is one of the primary causes of people not achieving the change they want in their lives. It keeps them trapped in the pain of regret, trying to do less of an unwanted behaviour, which in turn is a guaranteed way of maintaining focus on that behaviour and ensuring that it persists.

Reorientation occurs when we turn our attention to what it is that we **do** want, and orient our lives around that preferred behaviour. Saying to yourself that you need to stop eating junk food is only keeping the junk food in focus. Instead, focus on, visualise, and talk about healthy food, and let that become your orientation.

In essence, it's about accepting that we're all human and we all mess up. It's about recognising the special message regarding forgiveness that can be found within the Christian scriptures. The whole of the Easter period in the Christian calendar is about Jesus' message of forgiveness.

"Forgiveness is choosing to love. It is the first skill of self-giving love."

Mohandas K Gandhi

Chapter 2 Summary

Regret and resentment must be dealt with before one can achieve happiness. It's difficult to be happy or to seek to be happy if you're carrying baggage from the past. It's like going on a journey with a very heavy back-pack.

These festering emotions undermine our ability to live constructively in the present and maintain a good attitude. We all make mistakes, but we must leave them in the past and move on.

Choosing to forgive others and ourselves for past mistakes is the only way to let go of the baggage and reorient our lives to positive rather than negative behaviour.

"Do as the heavens have done, forget your evil; with them forgive yourself."

William Shakespeare

CHAPTER 3

Deal with the Present

Many of the great teachers of our times and of times past have placed a strong emphasis on peace and happiness being associated with living in the present or experiencing the present. Clearly, happiness has something to do with this present moment.

"Yesterday is history.
Tomorrow is a mystery.
And today? Today is a gift.
That's why we call it the present."

Babatunde Olatunji

---

1. Living in the Now

We have a past and we have a future, but we don't always live where we ought to, which is in the "now". **You and I have only the now, this present moment**. This is what we can each know about. We cannot do much about the past; it has already happened. We do not know if there will be a tomorrow. We can experience, however, and know about what is called the "now".

All you really have is now – the present moment. Now is now. What on earth do I mean about living in the now? How is this supposed to help in life?

So many of us make a very basic mistake in life in that we move out of the now and either try to **anticipate life and think or worry about the future**, or alternatively, spend time thinking, **worrying or perhaps feeling guilty or regretful about the past**. Think about it. You spend most of your life outside what is present and current and, instead, spend time worrying about the past and being overly concerned about the future.

"What I do today is important because I am paying a day of my life for it. What I accomplish must be worthwhile because the price is high."

Author unknown

Sometimes, for example, we retreat back into our head and we say things like, "If only..."

> ➢ "If only I hadn't said that."
> ➢ "If only I hadn't done that."
> ➢ "If only I'd made that deal."
> ➢ "If only I'd bought that property."
> ➢ "If only I'd taken that job."
> ➢ "If only I'd said 'yes'."
> ➢ "If only I'd spoken up."
> ➢ "If only I hadn't gone."

So let me ask you, if you kept on saying, "If only", how do you think you'd feel? Depressed. You'd feel down. You'd feel badly. So what's the solution? Stop the "If only" and stay in the present. Why torture yourself with a life of "If only"? Now is all you've got. Stay in the present.

On the other hand, we often say things to ourselves that start with "What if...?"

> ➢ "What if I mess up?"
> ➢ "What if I don't make it?"
> ➢ "What if I make a fool of myself?"
> ➢ "What if I'm no good at this?"
> ➢ "What if I don't succeed?"
> ➢ "What if I fail?"

Now, if I keep on asking, "What if", how am I going to feel? I'm going to feel bad, but what is the real emotion that I'm going to feel? Anxiety.

PAST	PRESENT	FUTURE
Depressed	Anxiety	
"If only..."	"What if..."	

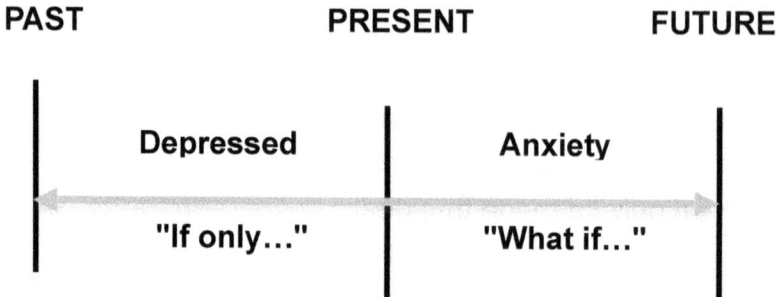

Interestingly, the psychotherapist Fritz Perls says that anxiety is experienced only when people step out of their present situation and retreat to the past, or worry about or try to anticipate the future. Clinically, anxiety fills the gap between the now and the future, and depression fills the gap between the now and the past.

So what's the real message here? The lesson is to stay in the now; stay in the present. What this means is that you will not be making dumb statements like, "If only," or asking those dumb questions like, "What if?"

Right now is fine. This moment is all that you know, all that you can really be aware of. You are just fine right now at this moment in time. It's a very important rule to be able to stay in the moment.

Living life in the now is one recipe for peace. As you experience your present moment, you have the potential for recognising peace. Of course, there are some present moments that do create tension, but usually they get worse when we think or worry about them excessively.

I'll check out the sunset later, I'm just leting everyone know how much I'm enjoying "living in the now".

Try a little exercise the next time you are tempted to move away from the present by thinking or worrying excessively. Look around you. Is there anything in the present moment to cause you concern? The answer is typically "No".

---

*"The only power you have
is the power of right now."*

Darryl Cross

"It's safe in this place right now. The walls are not falling in on me in this present moment; there's nothing to fear or to be concerned about." Living and appreciating the present moment also supplies us with more energy with which to live. It stands to reason that if you spend less time wasting energy living in the past or trying to live in the future, then you have more energy to experience what is happening right now.

In other words, you are not distracted by what has gone before or what you think might happen in the future. The principle is to be totally involved in what you are presently doing and enjoy the moment fully. It might even be something mundane like pulling up weeds, driving to the store, or washing dishes.

But being thankful for the present moment and enjoying – as though there were no tomorrow – is important! A wise priest once said, "Live today as though it were your last, and one day you'll be right."

Be thankful, for instance, for the fact that you can see, feel the breezes, hear the rain falling, drink in the scenery. Pay close attention to momentary pleasures and joys such as the sweetness of a juicy orange or the warmth of the sun on you. Decide that this present moment is for you to enjoy. Take time to smell the roses as it were.

Even if you are lawn-mowing, make each strip enjoyable. Maybe make it better than the last. Be thankful for the exercise and endeavour to make the most of it. This is one recipe for peace, happiness and contentment.

Living in the now and living every moment to its fullest means that we end up living life itself, without undue anxiety, and in the way we were intended. *The message is that it is important to live in the now, enjoying the present moment to the fullest, being thankful for each moment and making the most of it.*

2. Right Attitude

What is very powerful about "right" thinking, or positive thinking, is that it has a potent influence on living a satisfying life. Changing negative thoughts into positive thoughts is at the heart of the happiness journey. It's rather like that classic line from Shakespeare's Hamlet which reads, "There is nothing either good or bad but thinking makes it so".

Professor Martin Seligman, from the University of Pennsylvania in the USA, has discovered that feeling good and feeling positive, with a feeling of gratitude, actually extends life span. He cites at least twenty studies that show that **optimistic people live 8-9 years longer than negative people.**

Positive emotion lays down social capital in the form of greater life satisfaction, better relationships and fewer divorces.

As Henry Ford wisely wrote, "Whether you think you can or think you can't, you're right". There is a real sense in which you are what you think.

Check your attitude. It seems to be very natural and automatic for us to think the worst or think on the down side. "I wish...I should have...I don't need this...It's not fair...It's their fault...Why me?...Why now?...They're hopeless...They're deliberately trying to..." etc., etc.

"Success comes not from the way you think it does, it comes from the way you think."

Dr. Robert Schuller

The way you think is under **your control** (just like the way that you behave is under your control). So that means that you can do something about it! Here is **a principle you can follow**. Whenever you feel bad, check your thinking. Chances are that you are thinking "bad" thoughts. Stands to reason, doesn't it? Think happy thoughts…feel happy. Think angry thoughts …feel angry.

If you're smart and self-aware, when you feel bad (e.g., anxious, down, angry) you'll recognise that you need to turn your thoughts around. Reverse your thoughts, counteract them and see the situation from another perspective. You'll start to feel better. And life will become easier to handle.

"There are two sides to every coin – no exceptions."

Author unknown

Ask yourself, "Is the cup half empty or is it half full?" Is your situation a "problem" or is it an "opportunity"? Train yourself to see whether there is another side to your "coin".

Remember the story about the man who complained about his shoes, until he saw a man with no feet? Turn your story around, reverse it, counteract it, and look on the positive side. Yes, there *always* is a positive side. Always.

There is a fanciful story of identical twins. One was a hope-filled optimist. "Everything is coming up roses," he would say. The other twin was a sad and hopeless pessimist. He thought that Murphy, as in Murphy's Law, was an optimist. The worried parents of the two boys took them to see the local counsellor.

He suggested to the parents a plan to try to balance out the twins' personalities. "On their next birthday," he said, "put them in separate rooms to open their gifts. Give the pessimist the best toys that you can afford, and give the optimist a box of manure." They followed these instructions and carefully observed the results.

When they peeked in on the pessimist, they heard him verbally complaining, "I don't like the colour of this computer...I'll bet this calculator will break...I don't like this game...I know someone who's got a bigger toy car than this..."

Tiptoeing across the corridor, the parents peeked in and saw their little optimist gleefully throwing the manure up in the air. He was giggling. "You can't fool me! Where there's this much manure, there's gotta be a pony!"

What would it take for you to learn to think more positively, to see the cup as half full rather than half empty?[1]

3. Count Your Blessings

You've probably heard it before, but research supports this timely piece of common sense. At the University of California at Riverside, psychologist Sonja Lyubomirsky is using grant money from the National Institute of Health to study different kinds of happiness boosters. One is the "gratitude journal", which is a diary in which you write down things for which you are thankful.

She has found that taking the time to conscientiously count your blessings once a week significantly increased people's overall satisfaction with life over a period of six weeks, whereas a control group that did not keep journals had no such gain.

You simply write down three to five things for which you are currently thankful – from the mundane (your peonies or roses are in bloom) to the magnificent (a child's first steps).

Do this once a week, say, on Sunday night. Some of my clients do it daily and usually at night, as a way of

---

[1] For a full explanation of how to learn to see things in a more positive way, see my book titled, *"Stopping Your Self-Sabotage: Steps to Increase Self-Confidence"* available on www.amazon.com or www.amazon.com.au

reminding themselves not to take life for granted, and that indeed, life is good. Keep it fresh by varying your entries as much as possible.

Gratitude exercises can do more than lift one's mood. At the University of California at Davis, psychologist Robert Emmons found they improve physical health, raise energy levels and, for patients with neuromuscular disease, relieve pain and fatigue. He found that the ones who benefit most tend to elaborate more and have a wider span of things they're grateful for.

Look around you. What can you be grateful for on a daily or weekly basis? Remember, they don't have to be remarkable events, just the usual, the common; these tend to be the things that we overlook and that we need to remind ourselves of our fortune.

4. Practice Acts of Kindness

Another happiness booster, from the research of University of California psychologist Sonja Lyubomirsky, is that of performing acts of altruism or kindness – visiting a nursing home, helping a friend's child with homework, mowing a neighbour's lawn, writing a letter to a grandparent. Doing five kind acts a week, especially all in a single day, gave a measurable boost to Lyubomirsky's subjects.

These acts can be both **random** (let that harried mom go ahead of you in the checkout line) as well as

systematic (bring Sunday supper to an elderly neighbour).

A friend of mine related to me that one day on the way out of his parking garage, he told the attendant that he was also paying for the car behind him. You can imagine the surprise of the driver behind. Actually, I tried this when my wife and I drove from separate places to meet for shopping. On the way out of the parking lot, I told the attendant that I was also paying for my wife in the car behind. It sure made us both feel good!

Being kind to others, whether friends or strangers, triggers a cascade of positive effects – **it makes you feel generous and capable, gives you a greater sense of connection with others and wins you smiles**, approval and reciprocated kindness – all happiness boosters.

5. Thank a Mentor

Professor Seligman has tested various happiness interventions in controlled trials at Penn University and in huge experiments conducted over the Internet. The single most effective way to turbo-charge your joy he says, is to make what he calls a "gratitude visit".

In other words, writing a testimonial thanking a teacher, pastor or grandparent – anyone to whom you owe a debt of gratitude – and then visiting that person to read the letter of appreciation to them. Think about who in your life has had a profound positive impact on you. It could have been a manager or previous boss, a sports coach, a scout-master, an auntie or uncle – anyone who has impacted you significantly. If you can't visit because of the tyranny of distance, at least send it to them and perhaps phone to let them know that it is coming.

The research shows that people who do this just once are measurably happier and less depressed a month later, though the effect is gone within three months. Nevertheless, it is clear that it is worth doing.

If there's someone to whom you owe a debt of gratitude for guiding you at one of life's crossroads, or someone who has just been there for you, don't wait to express your appreciation – do so in detail and, if possible, in person. Besides, why wait until a person's funeral to say how important they were in your life?!

Less powerful, but more lasting, says Seligman, is an exercise he calls three blessings – taking time each day to write down a trio of things that went well that day and why.

The data shows that people are less depressed and happier three months later and six months later after doing this exercise. With that sort of research finding, why wouldn't you put it into practice?

6. Invest Time and Energy in Friends and Family

As we have hinted at already in Chapter 1, this is a big one. Virtually all the happiness exercises being tested by psychologists show that the over-riding theme to enhancing happiness is for people to feel more connected to others.

That seems to be one of the most fundamental findings from the science of happiness. Decades of research by Dr. Mihaly Csikszentmihalyi (pronounced "chicks-sent-me-high-ee") indicates that almost every person feels happier when they're with other people. In a sense, it's paradoxical, because many of us think we can hardly wait to get home after work and be alone with nothing to do. But that situation is actually detrimental to your well-being over time. If you're alone with nothing to do, especially for extended periods, the quality of your experience really plummets.

Friends and family is where your core is. That's where you will get most of your basic needs met, but not exclusively so. An elderly Anglican priest once told me a story. He said that he'd been at the bed-side of many people who had died. He'd been there in their final hours and final moments. He said that he'd never heard anyone say, "I wish I'd spent more time at the office". Instead, they would lament that they hadn't been a better dad or father, a better husband or wife, or a better mother or daughter. When it comes to the important things of life, it's usually about family and friends.

Longitudinal studies are rare, especially those that span 80 years. So, what does a longitudinal study across 80 years tell us about how to lead a good life and be successful in life? What secrets did such a study reveal about a satisfying life?

This study is reported by Dr Robert Waldinger who is a Clinical Professor of Psychiatry at Harvard Medical School and Director of the Harvard Study of Adult Development (see his TED Talk). He is currently the fourth Director of this project across four score years. The study began in 1938 where two groups of boys were studied from the Boston area.

One group were Sophomores (i.e., 10th grade in secondary school) from Harvard College and the other group were boys from a poor and disadvantaged area in Boston who lived in tenement housing with no hot or cold running water. Two very distinct groups.

Since the beginning of the study, these males have been interviewed every two years along with a range of assessments including medical reports, blood samples, brain scans, interviews with parents, and questionnaires. Once they moved into adulthood, the assessments also included videoing their relationship with their wives, as well as interviews with their children.

The study began with 724 men. Sixty are still alive and in their 90s. The research found that while some developed addictions such as alcoholism or developed mental health issues such as schizophrenia, others climbed the social ladder to the top. One in fact, was a US President.

How did some manage to struggle in life while others seemed to be very successful? The results were clear.

Firstly, it was discovered that **healthy connections** are positive for us as individuals. In contrast, loneliness creates a toxic environment where people are less happy, health declines earlier in mid-life, brain functioning deteriorates earlier and these people also live shorter lives. Within the USA at least, 1 in 5 persons report being lonely. What does that do for the health of a nation?

Secondly, it is not just about having friends or being in a committed relationship, it is about **the quality of those close relationships**. Living in a connected warm relationship is both positive and is protective. On the other hand, living in the midst of conflict such as a poor marriage, is bad for our health and is actually worse than getting divorced.

Interestingly, at age 50 years, the greatest predictor of health and satisfaction was **those who were engaged in a positive relationship**. Those most healthy in their 80s, were those most satisfied in their relationship in their 50s.

Thirdly, the research found that good, positive relationships not only protect our bodies, but also **protect our brains**. In other words, having secure and attached relationships where you can count on another person in times of need, when the going got tough, the other was there to support and care meant that our brain functioning in our 80s was significantly healthier. Those individuals who were in poor relationships had earlier memory decline.

So, one of the biggest happiness factors appears to be strong personal relationships, with family and friends, for example. As we've said before, the critical factor is working on social skills, close interpersonal ties and social support in order to be happy. Sure, you might be an introvert and less likely to be energised by people or or you might be single and not in a relationship, but irrespective, close ties are the secret to your happiness and contentment.

7. Take Care of Your Body

Getting plenty of sleep, exercising, stretching, smiling and laughing and having a good diet can all enhance your mood in the short term. We have already mentioned this in Chapter 1. Practiced regularly, they can all help make your daily life more satisfying. We all seem to know that it's just good common sense to look after ourselves. Well, the research backs that up. As they say, you lose it if you don't use it.

Living life is all about having energy. If you don't have energy for your day, you are starting well behind the eight ball. Is that not true? You've got to have the energy. Life is about energy, and if that might mean I have to go to bed early, then do it. We all know what sleep deprivation does to us from moodiness and irritability to impaired performance, poorer memory and judgment as well as reduced work efficiency. In the longer term, prolonged sleep deprivation leads to a host of health problems including obesity, diabetes, cardiovascular disease and even early mortality.

Health is about a proper diet and eating too. There is plenty of advice about appropriate eating habits including Mediterranean-style diets to other sorts of diets such as the Keto diet and plenty of advice about staying away from too much sugar and salt for instance. The Swedes for example, seem to be healthy lot in that they have a diet rich in oily fish, leafy vegetables, fruit and nuts.

Eating well and healthily provides a grand opportunity to live my day and live it well. If that means I have to watch what I'm doing and how I'm doing it, then I'll do that. It's critical. I want energy for my day, and that means taking care of my body. As Dr Michael Mosley, the British GP and TV presenter says, the best guide is to "keep a waist less than half your height".

Of course, exercise is also key. The basic rule seems to be to do something that gets your heart rate up three times a week for at least 20 minutes each time.

No surprises either, in suggesting that laughter and humour help here. With the stressors of life, it's tempting to get intense, be serious and carry on as though your life depends on it. While it is true that some things do demand a certain intensity, in the main, remember to laugh. It has been said that people who laugh, last the distance.

Try to be light-hearted as much as possible. It helps communication and it helps the level of tension in any situation. It means seeing the funny side of things, lightening up and sometimes laughing at yourself, too!

8. Being in the Zone

I have been at pains to say to all my clients, as well as to the MBA class that I teach, that all of us need to play to our strengths. What happens when you work to your strengths? Dr. Mihaly Csikszentmihalyi showed that real satisfaction occurs when we are "**in the flow**". Some call it being "**in the zone**". Prof. Seligman calls it the "**engaged life**" – being at one with the music, i.e., being totally absorbed in what you're doing so that time seems to stop. Dr Ken Robinson calls it being "**in your element**". In his book called *"The Element"*, it is defined as the meeting point between natural aptitude and personal passion. It's the place where the things we love to do and the things we are good at come together.

It's those times when you're so preoccupied that you lose track of time and you can't believe that time has really passed. Typically you're using your strengths and your talents and you're caught up in the activity. It could have to do with being involved with your hobbies or interests, or even romance and relationships. Maybe you're painting, writing, working on your car, giving a presentation, building a website, babysitting the grandchildren – whatever it is, you're "in your element". These activities give us energy rather than drain us (like our jobs often do). People become more alive because of these pursuits. There is little doubt that "being in the zone" increases happiness and satisfaction for people.

Do you know which of your strengths and talents have the effect of allowing you to be in your "zone"? When are you in your element? What do you need to do to experience more of being in your element?

Chapter 3 Summary

Worrying about the past or about the future can only distract us from the peace of the present moment.

This contentment and happiness can be found through having a positive attitude, keeping track of everything we are grateful for, practicing kindness, expressing thanks to others, spending quality time with friends and family, and finding our strengths and passion and then being truly engaged in what we are doing.

"Life can be found only in the present moment. The past is gone, the future is not yet here, and if we do not go back to ourselves in the present moment, we cannot be in touch with life."

Thich Nhat Nanh

CHAPTER 4

Deal with the Future

Of course, we all believe that there will be a tomorrow for us and that accordingly, we need to take account of what might occur for us there.

"The best thing about the future is that it only comes one day at a time."

Abraham Lincoln

As we've discussed, that doesn't mean worrying unnecessarily about what our future holds, or getting ourselves "into a stew" about it all, so what does it mean? How does happiness connect with our future? What does the research and clinical experience say about how we should approach our future in order to enhance happiness, our well-being and our success?

1. Living the Meaningful Life

Martin Seligman has a good deal to say about this notion of making a contribution and leaving a legacy. His work shows that one of the factors contributing to a satisfying, positive life is what he calls living a **"meaningful life"**. He has shown that the **largest contributor** to human happiness is belonging to and serving something bigger than ourselves; connecting with something external and using our higher strengths to serve something beyond our individual lives.

Of course, this makes total sense for those of us who are dedicated to our religious faith, but this finding is certainly food for thought for others of us. Religion seems to genuinely lift the spirit, and having faith in combination with the ability to surround yourself with a caring community is a powerful combination for happiness or a sense of well-being.

Seligman, in collaboration with Dr. Christopher Peterson at the University of Michigan in the USA, has focused on defining our strengths and finding new ways to deploy them. Using our strengths through giving makes us feel good about ourselves. When you're volunteering, you're distracting yourself from your own existence, and that's beneficial. Moreover, giving puts meaning into your life. You have a sense of purpose because you matter to someone else. Further information on this can be found at www.authentichappiness.org .

In my work as a career coach, many adults come in for coaching because they want a job or career where they can make difference. They want a job with some purpose and direction. In other words, they want a life that is meaningful. Whether that might be something about sustainability of the environment, saving the oceans, helping others grow and develop, creating something original, caring for certain sectors of the community like the aged or children or assisting in the protection and care of certain animals, they want to serve in some way and to feel that they are making a difference.

2. Develop Strategies for Coping with Hardships

There is no avoiding hard times. Religious faith has been shown to help people cope, but so do the secular beliefs enshrined in axioms like, "This too shall pass", and "That which doesn't kill me makes me stronger". The trick is that you have to believe them.

In short, Seligman argues in his 2002 book, *Authentic Happiness*, that there are three major components of happiness:

- getting more **pleasure** out of life (which can be done by savouring sensory experiences to give you the "smiley-face" experience) – i.e., being in the present and experiencing the now

- **engagement or being in the zone** (the depth of involvement with one's family, work, romance, interests and hobbies)

- **meaning** (using your personal strengths to serve some larger end, giving to others)

Of those three roads to a happy, satisfied life, **pleasure is the least consequential**. This is important to understand because so many people build their lives around pursuing pleasure alone. It turns out that **engagement and meaning are much more important**. As such, they act as buffers to what life has to throw at us and together with our mental attitude (see "Right Attitude" in Chapter 3), we are able to formulate important coping strategies.

3. Take a Risk (or Risks)

What's the point of tip-toeing carefully through life, only to make it safely to the grave? Life is not a dress rehearsal, as the saying goes. (I also remember someone once said, if somehow or other, you did manage to come back, you're not going to enjoy it because being dead really takes it out of you!)

So what's the message? Move out of your comfort zone and instead, move into your courage zone. Interestingly, once you move in any one direction out of your comfort zone, you automatically push out the courage zone in **all** directions. Eventually, your courage zone becomes your new comfort zone. And this is partly how you get self-confidence too.

Believe it or not, the real "juice" of life is lived in the courage zone. Conquering the courage zone makes people proud of themselves and gives them a sense of joy and achievement. Remember: *If you do what you've always done, you'll get what you've always got.*

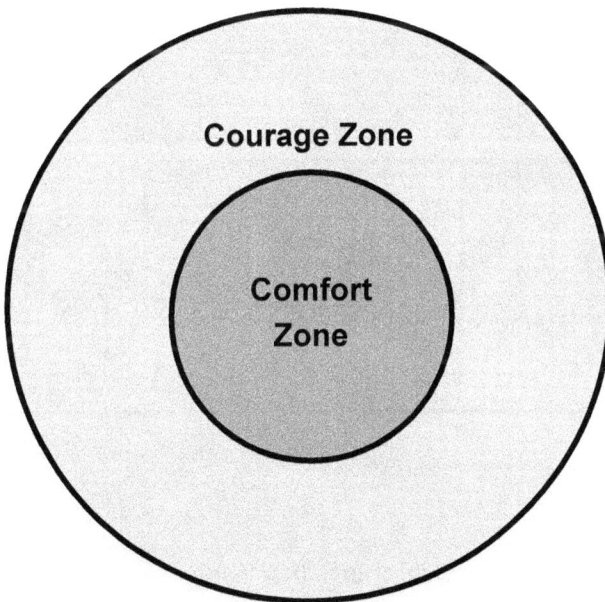

Life is about weighing the pros and cons, making a calculated decision, and then jumping off – but you have to jump. **Life rewards action.**

"Courage is an 'inside job'; but it's not something you think about, it's something you do."

Darryl Cross

The world does not reward you standing on the edge, procrastinating, blaming, feeling bad, making excuses – it could care less! If you jump off and you find that you are not falling in the right direction, life will always allow you to self-correct. Staying tied up at the dock does nothing to help you chart the course of your life. The learning is in the actual journey, where you manage the wind, the tides, and the odd storm. This is the real adventure of life.

You cannot change the direction of the wind, but you can adjust your sails. Of course, this statement presumes that you have cast off in the first place!

4. Set the Goals

Dr Edwin Locke from the University of Maryland, in a milestone piece of research on goal-setting across 30 years, using 40,000 subjects across 8 countries in both laboratory and field settings, and using more than 88 different tasks, showed without doubt that goal-setting is critical to your success and life satisfaction.

More particularly, the goals need to be specific and difficult, and it is helpful if you have someone to whom you are accountable and from whom you can receive constant feedback as to how you are progressing.

"People with goals succeed because they know where they are going."

Author Unknown

Your personal goal is like your road map. It ultimately points to your destination, e.g., what "career success" means for you; what "personal success" means for you; what you want to achieve. As someone once wrote,

Without your personal goal you are likely to:

- Experience uncertainty about the future.

- Experience a sense of gloom or depression about the future.

- Experience a sense of anxiety and possibly low self-esteem.

- Jump out of the frying pan into the fire.

- Not allow your unique talents to be used and to flourish.

- Settle for mediocrity rather than excellence.

With a personal goal you will be able to:

- Allow your priorities to keep you focused and on target.

- Identify more clearly what will motivate or inspire you.

- Find direction in the midst of constant change.

---

*"If you don't know where you are going,
how can you expect to get there?"*

Darryl Cross

---

5. Visualise Your Goals

Your picture becomes your guiding light. You are attracted towards that which you imagine. It almost becomes a self-fulfilling prophecy.

If you can't (or won't) see it in your mind's eye, don't be surprised when it doesn't happen. In life, there are two creations; first there is a mental picture, then there is the physical reality. No picture, no reality. That's just the way it is.

Your home was once simply a creation in the mind's eye of the architect. Builders didn't just arrive one day and start putting bricks and timber and steel together. They worked from a plan that was the creation of the architect. Mental picture: physical reality.

Wouldn't it be hard to do a jigsaw puzzle if you had no idea what you were creating and no picture to guide you? Typically the picture is on the lid of the box the puzzle comes in, and you need to have the picture next to you to work on it. You need to know what it will look like when you've finished.

In the same way, it's important to actually visualise how you would like to be (e.g., confident, happy, relaxed, successfully coping with change, leading your team effectively, being financially independent). Further, visualise what you would like to achieve (e.g., your specific goals, where you are going in life), and see it in your mind's eye. Picture it. See yourself making changes and doing things slightly differently.

Feel the emotion and start to live it and picture it in your thoughts. *If you can't (or won't) see it, don't be surprised when it doesn't happen.*[2]

---

[2] For more information on how to picture things in your mind's eye, visit www.amazon.com or www.amazon.com.au and purchase my book titled *"Stopping Your Self-Sabotage: Steps to Increase Your Self-Confidence."*

Florence Chadwick was the first woman to swim the English Channel in both directions. Now, at age 34, her goal was to become the first woman to swim from Catalina Island to the California coast.

On the 4th of July, 1952, she had been swimming for nearly 16 hours, but when she looked ahead, she saw nothing but a solid wall of fog. The sea was like an ice bath and the fog was so dense she could barely see her support boats. Sharks cruised toward her lone figure, only to be driven away by rifle shots. Against the frigid grip of the sea, she struggled on – hour after hour – while millions watched on national television.

Alongside Florence in one of the boats, her mother and her trainer offered encouragement. They told her it wasn't much further. But all she could see was fog. They urged her not to quit. She never ever had...until then. With only half a mile to go, she asked to be pulled out.

Still thawing her chilled body several hours later, she told a reporter, "Look, I'm not excusing myself, but if I could have seen land I might have made it." It was not fatigue or even the cold water that defeated her. It was the fog. She was unable to see her goal.

Two months later, she tried again. This time, despite the same dense fog, she swam with her faith intact and her goal clearly pictured in her mind. She knew that somewhere behind that fog was land and this time she made it!

Florence Chadwick became the first woman to swim the Catalina Channel, eclipsing the men's record by two hours!

Chapter 4 Summary

The work of Professor Seligman and other psychologists has shown that the largest contributor to human happiness is belonging to, and serving or connecting with something bigger than ourselves that gives meaning to our lives.

Living what is called the meaningful life is paramount to happiness and success in life.

In the same way, we can contribute to our happiness by having strategies that act as buffers to hardships so they don't cause setbacks, being adventurous and taking advantage of new opportunities and experiences in our courage zone, and establishing and visualising goals to keep us moving ahead and finding happiness rather than waiting for it to come to us.

CHAPTER 5

Time is a Matter of Priority

Anthony Robbins says that most people fail in life because they major in the minor things in life. So that brings me to the notion of time. What are you majoring in?

I don't know about you but I certainly have heard myself say things like, "There's never enough time". People in all walks of life are complaining that they are "time poor". This so-called scarcity of time makes them feel discontent and unhappy. It's almost like people are fighting time or struggling against time or against the clock. "Where has the time gone?" they say.

However, there are 86,400 seconds in a day, 24 hours in a day, and 168 hours in a week. You are not going to get any more. That's it; end of story – 168 hours a week is what you have to play with. But we often say to ourselves things like, "When I find the time". I'm sorry, but there's no more time to "find". It's 168 hours – there's no more, no less.

Charles Buxton once said, *"You will never find time for anything. If you want time you must make it".* Wise words. For people who say that they don't have enough time, I remind them that they have exactly the same number of hours per day that were given to people like Helen Keller, Pasteur, Michelangelo, Mother Theresa, Leonardo da Vinci, Thomas Jefferson, Albert Einstein, and anyone else you want to think about. You still have only 168 hours a week, just like they had. How you use it is what matters.

Time in Four Boxes

You may be familiar with Dr. Stephen Covey, a popular author, consultant and speaker, who wrote *The 7 Habits of Highly Effective People.* (If you haven't read that book, put it on your "to read" list; it's been a best seller for 25 years.) In that book, Covey said that there are two ways to really understand **time,** or two dimensions to time, namely, that which is **urgent** and that which is **important**. In other words, he said you can think about things being urgent and not urgent, and there are important and not important in regards to time.

According to your diary, your
schedule is the same as always . . .
9:00 am: Arrive at work.
9:05 am: Let the chaos ensue.

He said that when you divide time up into those two categories, you get some interesting patterns developing. You get four quadrants (see the table below).

In the **first quadrant**, you have things that are **both** urgent and important. These include crises, pressing problems, projects, and meetings that are deadline driven. This is where most people tend to live their day, especially in the work environment. Live all of your life in this quadrant though, and you become stressed, you become anxious and/or depressed and/or grumpy, irritable and angry, and sadly, you eventually burn out.

"Careful planning puts you ahead in the long run; hurry and scurry puts you further behind."

Proverbs 21:5

Going down the table is the **third quadrant** where things are also urgent, but **not** important. They might look important, but they really are not. Covey calls this the Quadrant of Deception. These include interruptions, some phone calls, some mail, some emails, some reports, some meetings – they may look like they are pressing matters, but they're not really. We tend to lose a good deal of time in this quadrant focusing on things that feign importance, but are not important. In a sense, we get conned and distracted by the unimportant

Then there is the **second quadrant,** in which matters are **not** urgent, but they are important. This is where you have to prepare things. You need to plan, prepare, create, think about things and work things out. This is where you take time out. You organise things, prioritise and set things in order. You work out what's important to do and what you value. You might manage risk and determine a Plan A and a possible Plan B for a situation.

Finally, in **quadrant four,** things are **not** urgent and they are **not** important. This is the Escape Quadrant. In this quadrant are things like trivia and junk mail and some phone calls. This is when people stand at the photocopier or the water-cooler and gossip at work, or surf the internet, or hang over the fence at home and talk about nothing or turn on the television and "veg" out.

In other words, they are time wasters, and Covey argues that if you live all your life in quadrant one, in the crises, then to escape you have to move down to quadrant four with the trivia. If you spend too much time in this quadrant at work, then you guessed it, you get fired.

"There is never enough time to do everything, but there is always enough time to do the most important thing."

Brian Tracy

	Urgent	Not Urgent
I m p o r t a n t	**I** • Crises • Pressing Problems • Deadline-driven projects, meetings, preparations	**II** • Preparation • Prevention • Values clarification • Planning • Relationship building • True re-creation • Empowerment
N o t I m p o r t a n t	**III** • Interruptions, some phone calls • Some mail, email, some reports • Some meetings • Many proximate, pressing matters • Many popular activities	**IV** • Trivia, busywork • Junk mail • Some phone calls • Internet surfing • Facebook, Twitter • Time wasters • "Escape" activities

Good Use of Time

Now let me ask you two questions. **What is the one activity that you know would have a significant positive impact on your *personal life* if you did it superbly well and consistently?**

What is the one activity that you know would have a significant positive impact on your *career* if you did it superbly well and consistently?

Think about these two questions. How would you answer them? Take a few minutes and write down your responses.

Let me suggest that your answers would typically fall into one of seven categories, namely:

➢ Improving communication
➢ Better planning and organising
➢ Taking better care of yourself
➢ Seizing the opportunity
➢ Better preparation
➢ Personal development
➢ Empowerment

If your answers did fall into one of these seven categories, then let me ask a further question. In which quadrant do these activities fall? Answer: Quadrant two. Quadrant two is important, but not urgent. That's where we do our preparation, our planning, our thinking. So, if all of those activities are in quadrant two, and they are important, why aren't you doing them?

More particularly, what would it take for you to invest more time in those quadrant two activities? Remember, these activities will have a significant positive impact on your personal and professional life. So, how would you organise yourself to get some quadrant two time? What would it take for you to schedule some regular planning time? What is stopping you from getting some creative thinking time? How could you get around those obstacles?

Finding quadrant two time gives people more control over their lives, gives them a sense of accomplishment, refreshes them, lifts their spirits, and re-energises them. Managing time and managing yourself in this way is a key to the pursuit of happiness. Isn't it worth doing?

I used to coach a partner in a law firm who would drive into the city each day, but en route, he would pull into a park overlooking lawns and gardens and spend 20 minutes thinking and planning his day. As it happens, he also did that on the way home so that he could get his head clear and not arrive home a grumpy old man. I also coached a partner in an architect firm who would go into the office each Friday as he normally did at 8.30am and be seen in the office for an hour or so before he'd tell his PA that he was going out for a meeting. He'd then go to a local coffee shop for at least an hour or more or to the local library to think and plan.

Where would you go for your planning time? How often and when would you go? How would you work it into your daily routine? How would you remember to fit it into your schedule? What would need to happen so that it became a habit?

Chapter 5 Summary

Many of us spend all our time putting out fires and meeting obligations. Then, when we absolutely must get away from these pressures, we fritter away our time on trivial pursuits. No wonder we say there's never enough time to do the things that are really important to us.

Instead, we need time to think, plan, build relationships, take care of ourselves, learn, and improve ourselves, and prioritising our time to be able to do these things will contribute greatly to our sense of satisfaction. Failure to use time wisely is a recipe for frustration and discontent. Happiness comes from mastering time rather than letting it master you.

"Half our life is spent trying to find something to do with the time we have rushed through life trying to save."

Will Rogers

CHAPTER 6

The Six Basic Human Needs

Much of your happiness lies in satisfying your basic needs. You have six, in case you didn't know. This framework was initially postulated by Anthony Robbins and I have found that it holds up well in everyday life. Let me tell you about your six basic needs, and let me reiterate that they need to be satisfied in order for you to find some happiness and success in life.

"Men take only their needs into consideration - never their abilities."

Napoleon Bonaparte

However, there is a qualifier, too: Each of these needs can be satisfied either in a positive way or in a negative way, so, of course, we want to approach them in a positive way. The first four needs are for survival; the last two needs are for fulfilment.

1. Security, Control and Sameness

The first need is **security and sameness or certainty and control**. You need to have some routine and control in your life. You need things to be fairly consistent, and maintain a sense of sameness. You need certainty and security. We like things to stay the same in order to avoid stress and to gain pleasure in life. In a sense, it's survival. We like to be certain about things and to be in control.

Think about a time when you were uncertain, when you felt insecure. Perhaps you were uncertain about your health, your finances or your children. It's likely that you were also unhappy at that time. So it's true we need security, we need sameness and control in order to feel more content.

To satisfy this need in a positive way, it is helpful to keep a diary or a PDA, and to manage your time effectively. To satisfy this need in a negative way is to be a "control freak" (and we probably all know someone who fits this label) or to be obsessive or compulsive. Managers and supervisors who are high on this need are micro-managers (and don't we hate this kind of style).

2. Variety

We also need **variety,** and we need different kinds of experiences in our lives. It's the other side of the coin, isn't it? It's the flip-side of the first need. Variety is the spice of life! In a sense, we need some uncertainty (as strange as that may seem). If you have sameness or certainty all the time, you are going to be very bored. In fact, **it has been said that the quality of your life is dependent upon how much variety or uncertainty you have in your life**. It's the juice of life.

To satisfy this need positively, we vary our lives. We take a vacation in a different place each year, go to different restaurants, travel to work by different routes, try different foods, meet new people, join a new group, try a new hobby and so on. Satisfying this need negatively, for example, is to binge on alcohol, take illicit drugs, gamble, have "one night stands," and so on.

3. Significance and Importance

The third aspect we need is to have **significance and importance** in our lives. There are a number of ways that we get a sense of significance and importance. It might be by achieving (e.g., gaining qualifications, getting a promotion, forging a career), or getting material possessions (e.g., clothes, homes, cars). In a negative way, people gain a sense of importance by tearing others down and being abusive, or on the other hand, they get noticed by playing "sick" or being "ill." They can also pursue this need negatively by living for goods and material possessions, having only designer-label clothes, driving only the latest BMW or Lexus, bragging about their latest trip to Europe or some exotic place.

Interestingly, though, the more that people become important and significant (e.g., going up the corporate ladder and gaining responsibility and power), the more isolated they tend to become and separate, and that brings us to the fourth need (which is the flip-side of the third need).

4. Love and Connection

We need to have **love and connection to someone else (e.g., your spouse, a friend) or perhaps something else (e.g., nature, your garden, a pet)**. It's all about relationships, connecting to others, bonding and communicating. Whether we like it or not, we are a gregarious people. We were built to interact and socialise.

This need therefore might be met through caring for or providing a service to someone else, being part of a friendship, or having a romantic relationship. For some people it might mean having and caring for a pet.

On the negative side, we might satisfy this need through gaining sympathy through sickness or injury, and playing "poor me".

As I hinted at above, because the need for connection is so strong, the leader or manager (or politician?) who becomes more important and significant in life usually lets work get in the way of his or her family responsibilities and therefore becomes dis-connected from the spouse and children. Because he or she still needs love and connection, they get "re-connected" by having an affair and usually to someone in their office or workplace.

This notion of being connected to others though is consistent with the research finding from Seligman and his associates that relationships with those around us are paramount to happiness. Whether it be with family or friends, connection with others is important to one's happiness and success. The research is very clear on this.

"The grand essentials of happiness are: something to do, something to love, and something to hope for."

Allan K. Chalmers

Satisfying these four needs therefore, will give you a sense of happiness if they are met in positive ways. However, *there are two more needs, and meeting these needs can provide fulfilment.*

5. Personal Growth

Personal growth and development is the fifth need. Life is about growth and learning. Anything on the planet that doesn't grow, dies.

It's about extending yourself, developing yourself, learning new things, and stepping out. It could involve reading, listening to a CD or a download on your mp3 player or i-pod or watching a movie on your i-pad. Maybe it's about learning a new skill such as public speaking or wood turning. Maybe it involves attending a vocational educational course or a set of lectures. My mother-in-law, for instance, who is in her 80s, recently attended a history course at the Third Age University for seniors, which she thoroughly enjoyed. My own parents in their late 80's have decided to finally learn to use a computer and attend various courses for seniors.

Fulfilling this need means trying new things, going to new places, and meeting new people – whatever it takes for you to extend yourself to learn and grow.

6. Leaving a Legacy

The final basic need which provides fulfilment when met is **leaving a legacy and making a contribution**. This is going beyond yourself; making a contribution to society and giving of yourself. That might mean that you join, volunteer for, or assist with a charity or community group. Perhaps it means giving money or assisting with fund-raising; giving of your time and/or knowledge; passing on skills or information. Maybe it means being a mentor to someone younger than yourself perhaps in your company or in the general community.

This sounds very familiar, doesn't it? This is parallel to Seligman's argument for happiness and satisfaction being associated with living a meaningful life.

In summary, in order to attain happiness and fulfilment, we need to make sure that we have satisfied all of these needs in our lives and in positive ways. We need to find ways in which to satisfy them, not only within ourselves, but in our family, in our work, and in our communities.

If we don't satisfy these six basic needs, we are lopsided. People who are lopsided are stressed and, needless to say, not happy or fulfilled.

Furthermore, if you think about those bosses who have been difficult to work for and who have caused you the most grief, chances are that they have majored in satisfying Need 1 (Control) and Need 3 (Significance & Importance). Without doubt, these bosses cause the most heartache in the workplace and are the cause of people leaving their jobs.

On the other hand, think of those leaders in the world who have made a substantial positive impact. For example, consider people like Nelson Mandela, Martin Luther King, Jr., and Mother Theresa. What needs would you say that they majored in? You guessed it. Need 6 (Contribution), Need 5 (Personal Growth) and Need 4 (Love and Connection).

What do we learn from this? The happiest bosses or leaders to work for are **not** those who are promulgating themselves and their egos through needs 1 and 3, but instead are concentrating on needs 4-6. Interestingly, and here's another paradox – those leaders who uphold needs 4-6 as a way of living, also receive needs 1-3 as a bonus! Now isn't that something to think about!

Chapter 6 Summary

It is important to understand that we have 6 basic needs that have to be satisfied in a positive way in order for us to not only survive, but to be fulfilled. Each of these needs can be played out within ourselves privately, within our family, at work or in the community.

Sadly though, the reason for our unhappiness is often that we either don't satisfy our basic needs or we satisfy them in negative or sabotaging ways. These basic needs which explain all our behaviour and point the way to happiness include the following:

1. Control / Security / Certainty
2. Variety / Uncertainty
3. Significance / Importance
4. Love / Connection
5. Personal Growth / Development
6. Leaving a Legacy / Making a Contribution

CHAPTER 7

Practical Tips

Tips are like handy guidelines. They are not rules. They are not laws. They are tips. It's important that you find out what works for you. As we well know, we're all different!

The following tips are not presented in any particular order. In a sense, they are a smorgasbord of suggestions and, as such, you can feel free to sample and taste wherever you like.

Of course, there may be nothing in the list that's to your liking, or nothing that strikes your fancy. However, there may be one or two morsels that you may like to try, and which may help you function better or help you in your pursuit of happiness.

Some of these tips in this chapter and the following might seem a little harsh or may offend. They are not intended to do so. They may cause some to hesitate. Try to understand the message underlying the suggestions. You are at liberty to sample what you will and you do not have to take on board anything with which you do not feel comfortable.

1. Next Day Planning List

Each night before bed, or each morning, make a list of what you have to do the next day, because if you haven't committed to your day in writing, it probably won't happen. Let me tell you very clearly, when you write things down, your brain gets it. Writing is very, very powerful.

Try to get into the habit of doing this at the end of the day. Some of my clients spend the last 10-15 minutes while they are at work to sort through their list for the next day.

Perhaps after dinner may be a good idea or just before bedtime (as long as it doesn't then keep you awake by thinking about it), but the more that you can introduce this task into a routine, the more likely it will be that you actually get things done.

2. Do Your Most Important Job First

Do your most important job first each day. Lots of us are procrastinators, aren't we? We kind of put things off and delay. There's a story about a steel manufacturing CEO from the United States who was given this idea by an employee, and he was so grateful that he sent his employee a check for $35,000. The CEO said, "This is how much doing the most important thing first each day has saved me".

Many of us get distracted first thing in the morning for example, with our emails and perhaps Facebook or Twitter. The minutes go by and before we know it, a half hour has gone or even more. Yet the morning is when we are freshest and have most energy, and hence, this is when we need to do the jobs that matter most. Emails and the like can wait.

3. Check Your TV Viewing and Screen Time

You may not necessarily like this message, but it has been suggested that you ought not to watch TV for more than about an hour a week. That's a tough goal if you like to watch, for example, football or some other sports, but, as I said before, it's about how you use your time.

A realistic goal might be to watch one or two shows per week that are the most important to you, and then try to find more fulfilling ways to spend the rest of those so-called TV-watching hours. The point is, that just sitting in front of the box for the sake of it does little to really provide satisfaction or fulfilment.

Same with the I-pad or touch pad. Certainly some clients have told me that they sit with their spouse in front of the TV as well as having the I-pad on their knee scrolling around and they wonder why their communication with their spouse isn't what it used to be and why they seem to be "ships passing in the night". Really?

Interestingly, Dr Jean Twenge, Professor of Psychology at San Diego State University has found that for teenagers, there are **two** activities that are significantly correlated with depression and suicide, namely, use of electronic devices (e.g., smartphone, tablet or computer) and watching TV. She found that when children and adolescents use screens for two hours of their leisure time per day or less, there is **no** elevated risk of depression. Above two hours per day, the risks grow with each additional hour of screen time. Sobering findings indeed.

On the other hand, she found that there were **five** activities that have an inverse relationship with depression (i.e., children who spend more hours per week on these activities show *lower* rates of depression). These include sports and other forms or exercise; attending religious services; reading books and other print material; in-person social interactions; and doing homework.

4. Check your Social Networking

Call it Facebook, MySpace, Linked-in, Twitter, Instagram or any other vehicle by which you keep in touch via cyberspace.

For many it has now become a recognised addiction while for others there is little doubt that it absorbs inordinate amounts of time.

Employers are now complaining that staff are checking their Facebook countless times during the working day interfering with the purpose for which they were employed. Teenagers rush home from school to see any updates on their site and that of their friends and then remain chatting or texting for the remainder of the night (and sometimes through the night).

For what? How did we keep in touch before Facebook or texting? Do we need to constantly be aware of what our Twitter friends are doing? Is catching up and spending prolonged periods of time on Facebook or Twitter our real purpose in life?

Do yourself a grand favour and put limits on both the number of times that you might check your sites and the amount of time that you spend on each site.

For example, you might want to check before lunch and then before bedtime; at least you then have set limits on how long you spend on each. Maybe limit it to once a day. After-all, you do have a life to lead.

5. Reward Yourself Every Single Day

We are good at beating up on ourselves and being self-critical (see my book *"Stopping Your Self-Sabotage"* available on www.amazon.com). Instead, it's important to reward yourself and daily too. Maybe it's a cappuccino. Maybe it's a relaxing bath. Maybe you do sit down for a half hour of TV. Maybe you pull out a book you've been wanting to read, but be good to yourself. Be kind to yourself. You're all you've got.

6. Keep Meetings Under 15 Minutes

A tip for running meetings: Circulate the agenda beforehand and conduct the meeting standing up. It's a great way to get through meetings! I left a job at a hospital some time back because of the kinds of time-wasters that John Cleese brings to mind in his training film called *Meetings, Bloody Meetings.* There were so many meetings. All those meetings finally got to me. I used to sit in the meetings and calculate the amount of money being wasted in wages for the sake of people just talking to hear themselves talk. I wish I'd known this rule back then!

I coach a principal in a pathology company and each morning they have a 10-15 minute stand up meeting around the kitchen table in the staff room. Everyone gets a sense about what is happening for the day and can report on the activities of the previous day.

Similarly, there is a young man I coach who is a fitter and turner by trade and he has instituted "tool box" meetings each morning where the workers stand around in a group to be briefed on what's on for the day and the day's priorities; it takes no longer than 10 minutes. He says it's invaluable in that it's short, employees know what is going on and it has cut down the mistakes that are made in the factory.

7. Spend Up To 30 Minutes a Day Thinking

Someone once said, "Thinking is the hardest work there is, which is probably why so few engage in it!" Those who spend time actually thinking for at least 15 minutes a day (and preferably 30 minutes) have an edge on others because they've done their homework beforehand, and have life a bit more in perspective. This is actually what effective leaders do, and we all are our own personal leaders. (Remember quadrant two in Chapter 5 as described by Dr. Stephen Covey.)

I've coached a number of leaders and individuals who have lamented that they don't have enough time to be able to sit and plan and think! Failure to do so inevitably means that you are handling more crises and putting out more fires that you need to do. I've coached a CEO for example, who has decided that each Thursday she will go into the office in the morning and then around 10.30am tell people that she was going out. She'd take the lift to the ground floor and walk around the corner to a coffee shop where she'd sit and think and plan for the next hour at least.

Put aside time to think. It directly helps in being able to control your life and get life more in balance.

8. Write Thrifty Replies

Reply to letters on the same paper that they were written on, and briefly. That is, of course, a business letter, not a personal letter. In a sense, it's what we do with emails anyway, so why not do it with hard copy as well!

"Our life is frittered away by detail...simplify, simplify."

(Henry David Thoreau)

---

9. Manage Your Emails

We simply don't seem to be able to get away from it. It is there 24/7. Whether the emails are addressed to us personally or whether we are simply copied in, they tend to hit our Inbox with rapid regularity.

I had a coaching session with a leader recently, and as she got up to leave, she glanced down at her smartphone and sighed that during our session, she'd received 29 emails. Almost every leader I know struggles with how to manage their emails and with trying to get the balance between getting back to people while at the same time managing their team and having the appropriate amount of interpersonal interaction.

Some leaders that I am aware of have a rider at the bottom of their automated response which says something along the lines that they will only be checking emails once or twice a day and therefore the sender ought not to expect an immediate reply.

10. Maximum of 4 Meetings in a Day with Gaps

If you are not able to limit your meetings to 15 minutes, then one of the most effective recipes for managing time that I have worked out with executives and leaders is this; limit yourself to a maximum of four meetings in a day, but more importantly, **ensure that there is at least a half-hour gap between meetings**.

If you really want to stress yourself and be ragged at the end of the day, then try for back-to-back meetings and cram the day with them. It is a sure-fire way to drain your energies quickly and to make sure that you become non-productive and ineffective.

I've seen it countless times.

The meetings are back-to-back, but they always seem to run over time. The leader is immediately stressed because the meeting has gone over and then arrives late to the next meeting without any time to collect their thoughts or get prepared. They arrive at the next meeting and due to the fluster of getting there late, it takes them 10 to 15 minutes to get their head right to participate in the present meeting. Of course too, they may well have had actions from the previous meeting which are now mounting up and will be added to the actions from the present meeting.

You can see how this mounts up and by the end of the day, the leader is completely frazzled or "fried".

11. Reduce distractions

We all have them, and these distractions all seem to vie for our attention. What can you do to eliminate these or reduce their impact? The best time managers will turn off their social media notifications, close down all unnecessary tabs on their computer and put their phone on airplane or flight mode.

Some bring in noise-cancelling head-phones into the office which are especially helpful in an open-plan office. Of course, you can always close your door (and even put a sign on it to say do not disturb – or words to that effect) or else book out an interview room to yourself to ensure some solitude while you work on an important matter. It's vital to do all you can to remove as many distractions as you can to assist you to concentrate and focus on what is in hand.

12. Plan Your Holidays

Plan your holidays at the beginning of the year. Why? What would be the advantage of that? It means that you have something to look forward to and gives you something to aim for. This gives a positive spin to your world, especially when the going gets tough. It's like having a light at the end of the tunnel.

Chapter 7 Summary

These practical tips might sound quite ordinary or in some cases quite strange, but they are designed to assist you in the pursuit of happiness.

CHAPTER 8

Psychological Tips

What are the tips that are of a more psychological or emotional nature that are important to keep in mind when striving towards success and happiness?

If anything, these are the tips that you really need to watch out for because failure to do so can directly sabotage your quest for happiness. Because some of these issues are not always conscious for us, they can slip under our radar and before we know it, we're feeling anything less than content and happy. The message? Overlook some of these tips at your peril.

1. Don't Sweat the Small Stuff (And It's All Small Stuff)

Isn't it true that we often focus on little problems and concerns and blow them out of proportion. In fact, clients typically come into my office and say, "I know it's only little, but..."

- In the total scheme of life, does it really matter?
- Is it worth it?
- Is it really a big deal?
- Is it going to make front page of the local newspaper?
- Are you going to allow them to continue to make you miserable?

A key question that I always ask people to consider is, **"Are you going to remember this incident in twelve month's time?"** Most answer that they won't even remember it in a week or two. Some say that they won't remember it in a day or two. So don't let it matter now. Keep life in perspective.

2. Let the Ball Drop; Don't Catch the Ball

Why do we own and take on board so many of the issues or problems that come our way? For example, someone calls us a name, gives us a label, and we **'own'** it. Someone throws you a concern and you automatically assume that you have to catch it and respond.

Maybe you think that you have to fix it, find a solution, or provide a remedy.

For example: Your friend calls and says, "My cousin is driving me nuts. What do you think I should do?" Typically, we automatically catch the ball and try to wade in and solve the problem. After we have expounded all our wisdom, our friend says, "Yes, but..." We then give more advice, only to be met with another, "Yes, but..." Why do we think we need to wade into it at all?

It takes two to tango! Just because your friend calls, doesn't mean that you have to take the bait. Say you'll get back later, or say that it really is for your friend to work out. Dropping the ball can really reduce the stress in your life.

When someone criticises you, puts you down, or throws a negative comment at you, you can catch it and feel hurt, or you can choose to let it drop and go about your business. Who says that they have a monopoly on the truth? It's only their opinion. Why take it on board?

"What you think of me is none of my business."

Author unknown

Just because it is thrown to you doesn't mean that you have to catch it. Think about it – and give yourself permission to let the ball drop.

3. Being Happy, Not Right

Do you want to be happy or right? Usually, you can't be both. Right and happy are often mutually exclusive. So what's the message here? Let others be right!

About 95% of our conflicts are not about facts or figures, but about opinions, values or feelings.

Being right means we have to defend our position. It takes a good deal of time and energy. It means that others get defensive, and it means that we strive to prove them wrong.

Somehow we see it as our duty to show others that their position, their point of view, or their opinion is incorrect, and that in doing so they are going to be so appreciative and eternally grateful to us. Know what? Yes, you guessed it. They're not appreciative at all! What makes you think that when you try to prove your point or show others how they're wrong, they are going to simply agree and give in to you? What makes you think that suddenly they are going to acknowledge that indeed, you are "the fount of all wisdom and knowledge and why hadn't they asked you before?" In fact, of course, the opposite happens. They dig in, they get defensive and argumentative, and they push back at you.

Sometimes, issues about your values or life philosophy are important enough to you that you may wish to express your perspective to the other person, but in the main, it is frequently more appropriate to just let others be right. Why not? Are you man or woman enough to let others be right? Or is your ego so frail that it has to be right and prove itself?

Change the way you correct people or tell them the "way it really is", and you'll find that your life will become less defensive and more loving, and people will appreciate you more, too. Gone will be the days of the battles of the egos – instead you'll be more at peace, and so will they.

4. Do People Feel Good in Your Presence?

Is the number of people who attend your funeral going to be determined by the weather forecast on that day?

Think of the people who have had the most positive influence in your life; those who perhaps have had the most profound impact on you personally. What traits or characteristics did they possess? How did they engage with you? What did they say and what did they do? Typically, they listened to you, challenged you, supported you, encouraged you, praised you, coached you. How did this make you feel? It made you feel cared for, important and special.

> *"The deepest human desire is to be appreciated."*
>
> William James

What would it take for you to do the same for others? Make other people feel important. Choose to be different. I remember someone once telling me that they imagined that every person they met or encountered had a sign across their forehead that read, "Make me feel important." They would then act accordingly. What a great attitude with which to approach others!

> *"It's amazing what you can do for someone who thinks their life is an accident when you treat them as if it were not."*
>
> John Fischer

5. Understand That Life Isn't Fair

Life isn't fair, so, don't expect it to be. Is it fair that an innocent person gets injured or killed by a drunken driver, or assaulted by a crazed robber? Is it fair that you get retrenched, divorced, ripped off by a colleague or friend? Is it fair that a loving mother who deeply cares for her children dies of cancer?

Sometimes life isn't fair. Sad but true. So don't sit around bemoaning the fact that it isn't. The sooner we understand that, and the sooner we get on with living, the better it is for us and those around us. It's not what happens to us that's important, it's what we do about it that's important.

6. Be Persistent

Keep going despite setbacks. Most of us, most of the time, are fairly quick to give up whenever we strike a hurdle. It's natural to do so. We immediately think that it's all too hard. Somehow we expect that it should all be easy and that things should just work out. Not so.

"Nothing in the world can take the place of persistence. Talent will not; nothing is more common than unsuccessful men with talent. Genius will not; unrewarded genius is almost a proverb. Education will not; the world is full of educated derelicts. Persistence and determination alone are omnipotent."

Calvin Coolidge

Instead, keep at it. When you receive feedback from your efforts and it's not what you expected or not what you wanted to hear, use it to refine your approach, but still keep going.

Anyone who has achieved success has had setbacks of some kind or other, and the mark of a champion is the person who keeps going and keeps persisting. Without exception, the countless leaders whom I have coached have hit hard times or difficult situations, but they have pushed through and they have persisted. It's easy to give up — that's why so many do it. It's the real leader who perseveres. Are you up for it?

Sir Winston Churchill took three years getting through his eighth year of school because he had trouble learning English. (Today we call it a learning disorder.) It seems ironic that years later Oxford University asked him to address its commencement exercises for the start of the academic year.

He arrived with his usual props. A cigar, a cane, and a top hat accompanied Churchill wherever he went. As Churchill approached the podium, the crowd rose in appreciative applause. With unmatched dignity, he settled the crowd and stood confident before his admirers. Removing and carefully placing the top hat on the podium, Churchill gazed at his waiting audience. He then shouted with authority, "Never give up!"

> *Several seconds passed before he rose on his toes and repeated, "Never give up!" His words thundered in their ears. There was a deafening silence as Churchill reached for his hat, steadied himself with his cane and left the platform.*
>
> *Three words only and his commencement address was finished.*

7. Action Not Good Intentions

In life, it is important to make careful decisions and then let the arrow fly. Understand that the world couldn't careless about your thoughts if there are no actions.

"Life rewards actions, not good intentions."

Darryl Cross

People don't care about your intentions. They care about what you do. The tax office doesn't care if you "meant" to pay your taxes. Your child doesn't care that you "meant" to get dinner. The pedestrians at the pedestrian crossing are not at all comforted that you "meant" to stop. The police department could care less that you "meant" to pay your fine. The planet could care less that you "thought" about losing weight, that you "thought" about becoming more confident, that you "thought" about taking a course, that you "thought" about taking a risk. The planet could care less what you intended to do. It only rewards your action – what you actually physically do. What matters, what determines the script of your life, is what you actually **do**.

"Life is like riding a bicycle – you don't fall off unless you stop peddling."

Claude Pepper

Procrastination (i.e., mere intention) is the bane of human existence. Successful people, instead, take purposeful, meaningful action. They don't just think about it. They don't plan themselves to death. They don't have a meeting to plan a meeting to set up a meeting to decide what to do.

They also realise that if they take an action and it turns out not to be the correct action, that they can take a further action to re-correct. Like a yacht, they know that they don't go straight towards their target. Instead, they tack towards their destination, correcting and re-correcting according to the prevailing conditions, but always sailing forward.

"All glory comes from daring to begin."

Eugene F. Ware

Successful people don't procrastinate, they begin. As they begin, they gain a momentum like the flywheel. It takes effort to get going initially, but once it has momentum, it has its own energy keeping it going.

If you begin to do something, whether it's exercising, giving your feelings a voice, going back to school, praying, meditating, or applying for a new job, your actions will gain momentum. You'll meet new people; new possibilities will open themselves to you.

Soon enough, you'll discover that your life is no longer the same sing-song. You'll realise that those old sayings have long lives because they're true: "You can't get a hit if you're not swinging", "You can't catch a fish if you don't put your hook in the water". This principle is about getting you to swing the bat or cast your line. It's about putting some verbs in your sentences and action in your life.

"The pain of discipline is measured in gms.
The pain of regret is measured in tons."

Author unknown

8. Take Responsibility for Your Life

Understand that you have to take some responsibility for your life. You are in charge. I like the quote by Woody Allen: *"Eighty percent of success is showing up"*. In other words, it's what you do – for just showing up you are 80% there. So taking responsibility for living is an important clue to striving towards happiness.

Do you know the definition of stupidity? It's doing the same thing day after day and expecting a different result. So instead, it's about making choices for yourself and not simply doing the same ol' same ol'.

Taking responsibility for yourself means not getting caught up in the blame game. Who is there to blame? "It wasn't me." It is always someone else; it's someone else's fault. But who really is driving the bus? Are we going to blame our parents? Are we going to blame our upbringing, our spouse, our children, our education or our teachers? I'm not suggesting that some of these areas weren't tough ones in your past. I've been around for thirty-plus years in my profession, and I know some of these issues are difficult to resolve. Family issues, for example, are particularly thorny ones.

Our upbringing can be tough, so can our work environment, our boss, or management – they always get it wrong somehow, don't they, in every organisation. Perhaps we can blame policies, legislation or politics in the community. But who really is in control here? Us. And we need to take responsibility.

We need to make decisions and we need to make choices. Take responsibility. Own your decisions and own your life.

9. Keep the Main Thing the Main Thing

Ever heard of the 80:20 rule? It's sometimes called the Pareto Principle named after Vilfredo Pareto who was an Italian economist. When he discovered the principle, it established that 80% of the land in Italy was owned by 20% of the population.

Later, he discovered that the Pareto Principle was valid in other parts of his life such as gardening where 80% of his garden peas were produced by 20% of the peapods.

Think about your own life and circumstance:
* 80% of your rewards comes from 20% of your activities
* 80% of your problems come from 20% of the people in your life
* 20% of your friends provide 80% of the real support and companionship in your life

What about in the world of work and business?
* 20% of your customers provide 80% of your sales
* 20% of your products provide 80% of your sales

- 20% of your customers provide 80% of your profit
- 20% of your products provide 80% of your problems
- 20% of your customers provide 80% of your problems
- 20% of your staff cause 80% of your issues

So what is the lesson here? Focus on what's really important. Don't be distracted by the 80% of peripheral fringe that doesn't give you the reward or success that is yours. Don't get waylaid into detours or back alleys that simply take your time and energy, but don't give you what you want. Don't go along with the crowd or your peers when it takes you away from your real purpose or direction. Keep the main thing the main thing.

Work out what your 20% is and keep focusing on it. Is it a special relationship, a course, a hobby, a job role or function? What is it that gives you that success that you're after? It will be in the 20% area; so find it and focus on it.

10. Some Things You Can Change and Some You Cannot

I heard someone recently give some very wise advice. He simply said this: "There are some things that you can't change." We can't control the weather, and if it's raining, well, it's raining. That's just the way it is. Now if that's so, and we can't change some things, then why worry about them? That's a valid question, isn't it? There are certain things that are beyond our control, so why worry about them? I can think of no reason to worry on that score, and I kind of like that logic. Nice.

This same person went on to say, "You know, there are some things that you **can** change, and if that's so, why worry about them, because you can actually change them?" I thought that sounded pretty good logic, too.

Then I said to myself, "Well, if there are some things I **can't** change and I don't have to worry about them, and there other things I **can** change and I don't need to worry about them, what is there left to worry about?"

So, let me ask you, what **is** there left to worry about?

11. Life is Never a Straight Line

I almost always watch the start of that great classic boat race, the Sydney to Hobart challenge which always begins on the day after Christmas Day. This annual Sydney to Hobart Yacht Race is one of the most prestigious races in the world yachting calendar and attracts boats and crews from all over the world. The 2,000km (1,240 miles) race sees yachts race out from Sydney Harbour trying to make the fastest time south to Hobart in Tasmania. First held in 1945, the Yacht Race is a huge post-Christmas tradition that always generates huge public and media interest.

I don't know much about yachting though. However, what I do know is that to get from A to B (or from Sydney to Hobart or wherever), these yachts never go in a straight line. Why? Well, there are the winds, the tides, the currents and the occasional storm. They tack to their destination. They zig-zag to their port.

So it is with us. You may have a career goal, a financial goal, a health goal, a life goal. It may a short-term goal or a long-term goal. Whatever it is, *be prepared to tack to your destination.* This is important to understand. So many of my coaching clients remain tied up at the wharf unwilling or scared to cast off because they can't see a direct straight line to their goal. But there is no straight line. It's always a tacking process. It takes a risk to cast off and then to be aware on the journey of the winds, the tides, and the odd storm.

Don't look for the straight line or for "all the ducks to line up" before you start your journey. If you wait for all the details to be clear, you'll never leave the wharf. All you'll really know is the weather for today and the next few days. All you know is the next step, the next tack. Once you're on the journey towards your goal, you'll work out when to tack next and what the next step is. It's an on-going evaluation and feedback process. You just need to be heading forward and in the direction of your goal.

I once heard a speaker remind the audience about the Apollo spacecraft that went to the moon. He then asked the question, "How much of the time do you think that the

Apollo craft was on target as it headed towards the Moon with those astronauts on board?" The audience gave various responses, 90%, 85%, 75%, and so on. He waited a short while and in the silence, he wrote up on the whiteboard the figure of 3%. Only 3%? Now it may well be that it was actually more than that, but irrespective, the point he was making is that if the spacecraft was only directly on target a small percentage of time, what was it doing the rest of the time? Self-correcting. Yes, evaluating its position and correcting.

That's how it is with us. You can't know what "weather" life will throw at you and you can't predict the winds and tides of life. What you do though, is cast off and read the elements as you journey and be prepared to self-correct and tack.

Interestingly too, often it is the smallest tacks that can bring about a surprise event. You just never know. Further, many of my clients have stated that as they progressed in the journey towards their goal (whatever that was) and as they got closer, they were in a better position to realise that their original goal was not what they really desired and they were able to refine the goal and change direction accordingly to a newer better goal.

The real lesson though is to be brave enough to cast off and then be prepared to navigate your way, making various tacks as you assess the environment around you. Understand that you never travel in a straight line. Never.

Chapter 8 Summary

There are lots of ideas out there about how to achieve happiness. You may find many of the psychological tips provided in this chapter to be great ways to boost your outlook, improve your attitude, and keep happy thoughts front and centre.

CHAPTER 9

The Final Word

Unlike the animals, who seem quite content to simply be themselves, we humans are always looking for ways to be more than or other than what we find ourselves to be. We explore the countryside for excitement, search our souls for meaning, shop the world for pleasure. We try this. Then we try that. The usual fields of endeavour are money, sex, power, adventure and knowledge.

Everything we try is so promising at first! But nothing ever seems to amount to much.

> *We intensify our efforts – but the harder we work at it, the less we get out of it. Some people give up early and settle for a humdrum life. Others never seem to learn, and so they flail away through a lifetime, becoming less and less human by the year, until by the time they die there is hardly enough humanity left to compose a corpse.*
>
> *Introduction to the Book of Ecclesiastes, the Bible; Message translation by Eugene H Peterson.*

So what's it to be? How will you lead your life? Will you simply survive and die with your "music" still in you? Or will you seek to thrive and be fulfilled reaching toward being your best and seeking success and happiness for yourself?

The fact that you have read to this point in the book indicates that you seem motivated to do something about your life and the way that you live it.

I really like the saying that you can't change the direction of the wind, but you can adjust your sails; yes, you can adjust your sails.

I like the notion that although it is difficult to suddenly arrive at your destination, you can at least change your direction and head towards where you want to go. And it's **not** about getting there in a hurry, it's about getting there enjoyably, having the choice to change direction when you want to, taking a different tack, and taking it one step at a time.

"Step by step, day by day, achievers do what non-achievers don't bother to do."

Author unknown

Finally, all of this is going to need some **discipline**. Discipline. Yes, some people call this a "dirty" word, but Jim Rohn once said that "Discipline is the bridge between goals and accomplishments". You need to make it happen. This is exactly where so many give up and the minority succeed. This is where the few put in the effort and the majority sit back and do nothing or worse still, complain, blame and make excuses. Then when the minority make it, they say things like, "aren't they lucky!" Luck? You make your own "luck" by putting in the effort. As the golfer Gary Player once said, "The harder I work, the luckier I get".

There is in this world, a gap between the "knowing" and the "doing". In other words, lots of the population know what to do, but do they actually do it? Indeed, it is a mark of the successful person that they bridge the gap between what they know ought to be done and actually following through. They actually do things. They actually get up and make it happen. They may not feel like doing it, but they go ahead and do it anyway. If I waited until I "felt" like going down to the gym to workout, I'd never go. The hallmark of the successful person, is that they just go and do it anyway.

"Great things are not done by impulse, but by a series of small things brought together."

Vincent van Gogh

It's the same in business too. There are the training programs and the strategies that might be provided and outlined, but the implementation falls over. There is no follow through. What a waste of time and effort. What a way to damper morale.

Talk is cheap. You know that as well as I do. It's easy to talk. We're good at it. However, **life rewards action**, as I mentioned before. This is where the rubber really hits the road. This is where the men and women step up, while the boys and girls slip away.

So what is the one thing that you will take away from reading this book? What will you do differently tomorrow? But how will you do it? What is your next step? Is it making a phone call? Actually sitting down and making a plan?

More particularly, **how** will you remember to do this next step? What visual prompts or reminders will you put in place to actually get started? Having a good intention will not do it. You'll forget and you'll get distracted by the busy-ness of life. And besides, your old habits will kick in and you'll be a slave to your previous routine. Instead, help your brain out by getting a visual prompt. A client of mine had post-it notes on their mirror in the bathroom to constantly keep things in focus. Another client bought a new pen which acted as his prompt to do things differently. Still another bought a new watch band.

Further, **who** will keep you accountable on this next step and the steps beyond? Will it be a friend? Will you hire a coach? How often will you meet to "report in?" It's easier for me to get down to the gym if I know that my personal trainer is there waiting for me. You need someone to keep you accountable. Successful people almost always have a mentor, coach or trusted ally. Who will it be for you? What is your next step to make this happen? A phone call, an email, a conversation?

"You cannot change your destination overnight, but you can change your direction overnight."

Jim Rohn

You owe it to yourself to be on the journey towards success and happiness. You're worth it.

ABOUT THE AUTHOR

CROSSWAYS COACHING

**Dr. DARRYL G. CROSS
PhD (Psychology)**

**Psychologist,
& Leadership Coach**

*Fellow, Australian Psychological Society
Fellow, Institute of Managers and Leaders
Certified Personal & Executive Coach, College of Exec.Coaching
Member, International Coach Federation
Member, Career Development Association of Australia
Graduate Member, Australian Institute of Company Directors
Accredited Advisor, Family Business Australia
Accredited Facilitator, Mindshop Australia Ltd
Foreign Affiliate, American Psychological Association
Registered Psychologist*

Dr. Darryl Cross is both a **clinical and organisational psychologist**, a personal and executive coach, and an author, international speaker and sessional university lecturer.

Darryl completed his Psychology Honours Degree in Psychology at Flinders University, South Australia. He gained his Doctorate in Psychology from the University of Queensland.

More recently, Darryl completed a Professional Development Certificate in Coaching Practice through the Department of Psychology at the University of Sydney, and then completed graduate studies in coaching with the College of Executive Coaching in California, USA.

He **knows how organisations work** from his first appointment for three years as an Occupational Psychologist with the Australian Federal Government. He was the director of a hospital department in Adelaide before starting his own consulting business twenty years ago.

As a **university lecturer**, Darryl tutored and lectured in psychology at the University of Queensland in Brisbane for seven years, and lectured in the post-graduate programs in psychology at Macquarie University in Sydney, New South Wales for three years. He was a sessional lecturer in Leadership Dynamics in the MBA Program in the International Graduate School of Business at the University of South Australia and at Torrens University.

As a **speaker**, Darryl has conducted countless workshops on numerous topics, including training managers and leaders as coaches, increasing self-confidence, dealing with conflict, and the art of listening.

He has spoken internationally at numerous conferences and symposia, and has presented workshops in countries such as the United Kingdom and the USA, and in Southeast Asia.

As an **author**, Darryl has published numerous papers for national and overseas academic journals, as well as articles for the popular press. He has also authored books such as: *"Listen Up Now! How to Increase Profit and Growth in Business by Really Listening to Your Clients & Customers."*

Other titles on **www.amazon.com** and **www.amazon.com.au** include:

"Growing up Children: How to Get 5-12 Year Olds to Behave & Do As They're Told"

"Teenager Trouble-Shooting: How to Stop Your Adolescent Driving You Crazy"

"Stopping Your Self-Sabotage: Steps to Increase Self-Confidence"

"The Dark Clouds at Work: How to Manage Depressed Staff in the Workplace Whilst Increasing Morale & Productivity"

"You're a New Leader: So Now What?"

Darryl is heard regularly on talk-back radio in Australia, and is often seen in various segments on television as well as in the print media. He knows what he's talking about, and is called upon to give his opinion.

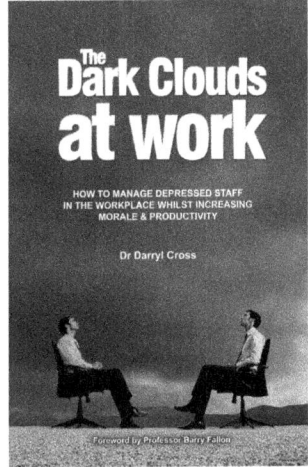

Academic study, life experience, and being a psychologist and coach for over thirty years, means that Darryl has come up with practical ways to use principles of life that work. He understands human behaviour and therefore can help individuals and teams to move to another place. He has the knack of being able to say it all simply.

Address: Crossways Consulting
PO Box 2000,
North Adelaide
South Australia
AUSTRALIA   5006

Email: enquiries@crossways.com.au

www.DrDarryl.com

www.LeadershipCoaching.com.au

www.FindACareerPath.com

www.MyFutureCareer.com.au

www.GrowingUpChildren.com

www.TeenagerTroubleShooting.com

www.CyberSafetyDoctor.com.au

www.HowToStopSelfSabotage.com

www.DepressionAtWork.com

www.ListenUpNow.com.au

www.SuccessPursuit.com

www.ingramcontent.com/pod-product-compliance
Lightning Source LLC
Chambersburg PA
CBHW072142020426
42334CB00018B/1858